THE HOUSE OF MODERATE COST IS NOT ONLY AMERICA'S MAJOR ARCHITECTURAL PROBLEM BUT THE PROBLEM MOST DIFFICULT FOR HER MAJOR ARCHITECTS.

—FRANK LLOYD WRIGHT

THE NATURAL HOUSE, 1954

FRANK LLOYD WRIGHT'S USONIAN HOUSES

⊞ CARLA LIND ⊞

AN ARCHETYPE PRESS BOOK
POMEGRANATE ARTBOOKS, SAN FRANCISCO

Library of Congress Cataloging-in-Publication Data

Lind, Carla.

Frank Lloyd Wright's Usonian houses / Carla Lind.

    p.   cm.

"An Archetype Press book."

Includes bibliographical references.

ISBN 1-56640-998-5

1. Wright, Frank Lloyd, 1867–1959 — Criticism and interpretation. 2. Usonian houses — United States. I. Title.

NA737.W7L54 1994   94-7934

728'.373'092–dc20   CIP

Published by Pomegranate Artbooks

Box 6099, Rohnert Park,

California 94927-6099

Produced by Archetype Press, Inc.

Washington, D.C.

Project Director: Diane Maddex

Art Director: Robert L. Wiser

Asst. Art Director: Marc A. Meadows

10 9 8 7 6 5 4 3 2 1

Printed in Singapore

Opening photographs: Page 1: Frank Lloyd Wright at Usonia in Pleasantville, New York, in 1952. Page 2: The living room of the Tracy house, a Usonian Automatic design.

CONTENTS

DURING THE GREAT DEPRESSION of the 1930s and in the years following World War II, America was faced with a major architectural problem: the need for good, moderately priced housing. Frank Lloyd Wright was determined to find a solution. He was convinced that a low-cost residence should reflect contemporary needs rather than be a small imitation of a grand house. He applied his principles of organic architecture to the problem and developed the Usonian house—a continuation of his lifelong quest to destroy boxlike rooms, to wed a building to its site, to simplify the parts of a house, to use materials and technologies in innovative, honest ways, and to build to suit democracy.

Wright (1867–1959) coined the term *Usonian* to describe the residents of a culturally reformed United States of North America. He used the name broadly to describe most of his 140 houses constructed from 1936 until his death in 1959. Some of these were far from small, modestly priced residences. But even the large, expensive houses were based on many, if not all, of the original

Inside and out, dominant horizontal lines shape the Rosenbaum house of 1939 in Florence, Alabama (pages 6–7). Built-in furniture (opposite) ensures the most efficient allocation of limited space.

Usonian fundamentals that enabled the owners to "get more for their money."

Wright first presented his Usonian manifesto in *Architectural Forum* in 1938 (and later in *The Natural House* of 1954). His faltering career was reborn, with the Usonian house as the centerpiece of his vision for decentralized, nature-oriented communities, which he called Broadacre City. While the vast majority of Wright's Usonian commissions were for individual houses, he was

A model Usonian house built in New York City in 1953 allowed Wright to bring his Usonian principles to a large audience. Raised on the current site of the Guggenheim Museum, it was the centerpiece of a retrospective of Wright's work.

able to use some of his community planning concepts for cooperative enclaves in Michigan and New York State during the 1940s and 1950s.

Wright was always eager to share his ideas with young people and encouraged do-it-yourself participation in the houses he designed. Not only did it save money; it also connected clients spiritually to their home, increasing its significance in their lives. While Wright professed that it was necessary for an architect to be involved in each design, he also explored standardization and prefabrication at various times in his seventy-year career. Each of the Usonian commissions was assigned to an apprentice who could make the countless on-site decisions.

Wright's Usonian house innovations helped change the course of small house construction in the United States. His simplification of the form and emphasis on spaciousness rather than space altered the face of suburbia as one-story horizontal plans, open kitchens, carports, window walls, and patios became mainstream. Wright believed that his houses, regardless of size, gave their owners a sense of dignity and pride in their surroundings.

❖❖ I saw a house, primarily, as a livable interior space under ample shelter. I liked the *sense of shelter* in the look of a building. ❖❖
Frank Lloyd Wright
The Natural House, 1954

To increase the sense of spaciousness in the compact Goetsch-Winckler house, Wright designed each room so that it opens to an outside terrace or patio.

Dominant horizontal lines

Houses that are companions to the earth and more human in scale

Flat roofs with large overhangs

Roofs that protect walls and provide shelter, usually light colored to reflect light inside

Standardized natural materials

Less expensive materials that look like what they are—wood, brick, concrete, and glass—and required little custom labor on site

Unit system walls

Walls that are the same inside and out—a sandwich of three thicknesses of standardized, machine-sized boards with paper between them and screwed together. Later, a system of concrete blocks

Integrated windows

Rows of casement windows. Distinctive cutout clerestory patterns. French doors opening to patios

Organic siting

A private side and an open side, usually facing south

Carports

Roofed but open areas, integrated into the design, instead of garages

Modules

Floor plans and overall designs based on a grid like Wright's childhood Froebel blocks

Zoned plans

Three primary areas: living spaces, kitchen-dining areas at the intersection, and small bedrooms

Open living areas

Open plans featuring views to the garden, with a central fireplace

Adjacent cooking-dining areas

Dining spaces and kitchens ("workspaces") next to the living area

Service cores

Utilities housed near the kitchen, perhaps a small cellar for heat, fuel, and laundry

Concrete slab floors

Red floors marked with an incised grid like the overall house module

Integral gravity heating

Pipes placed beneath the slab floor to carry hot water or steam, which rises to warm the rooms

Top: The flat, overhanging roof of the **Affleck house** and perforated window screens at the **Pope-Leighey house**. Bottom: The **Hanna house's** French doors and its unit wall system.

Simplicity above all

Elimination of all that was unnecessary for the sake of efficiency: separate furniture, bric-a-brac, individual light fixtures, radiators, trim, paint, and plaster

Integral decoration

Features integrated into the design through manipulation of the building materials themselves

Modular furniture

Components often built on site, using the same module, grammar, and materials as the building

Built-in components

Sofas, benches, bookcases, cabinets, and tables designed to coordinate and conserve space

Freestanding pieces

Tables, chairs, and stools combined for different uses

Inexpensive materials

Plywood, like the house's exterior cladding, frequently employed

Inside-outside walls

Textures carrying the exterior building materials inside: board-and-batten walls of pine or cypress, masonry, or concrete block

Perforated wood screens

Geometric patterns to filter light through windows and create shadows. Designs reflecting the thematic module of the house

Central hearths

Tall masonry fireplaces that provide an anchor for open living spaces

Warm colors

Cherokee red and soft golds predominant, with some yellow-greens and blues introduced in later years

Indirect lighting

Concealed fixtures reflecting off the ceiling, some casting patterns from beneath perforated shades

Simple textiles

Natural fibers and textures, often handwoven, with no patterns except natural weaves

Accessories

Limited decorative objects such as weeds, branches, useful pots, and Oriental artifacts

Top: The Palmer house's triangular floor module and custom furniture in the Rayward-Shepard house. Bottom: Integral lighting at the Smith house and the Hanna house's central fireplace.

JACOBS HOUSE I

MADISON, WISCONSIN. 1936

RECOGNIZED AS THE FIRST EXECUTED Usonian house, this residence for Herbert and Katherine Jacobs was completed for a mere $5,500. Wright closely watched the construction and the cost of this small home because of its significance and its proximity to his own house, Taliesin, in nearby Spring Green.

The informality and efficiency of Wright's open plan suited the young family. Its L-shaped design is open on one side to a private garden area but closed on the street side. Tall casement windows and doors open out from the living room and both bedrooms. At the junction of the bedroom and living room arms is the workspace kitchen. The house's 1,340 square feet were based on a rectangular module whose grid, scored into the concrete slab floor, was the basis for all design decisions. The horizontal grounding of the Jacobs house to its site seems as natural as the materials from which it was built—the vertical window and fireplace elements pinning it in place.

The Jacobses were so happy with their home that they commissioned Wright to design a larger one for their expanded family just seven years later.

⠿ ... home means more than money and the smaller means sometimes show the best results. ⠿

Frank Lloyd Wright
The Architect and the Machine,
1894

Board-and-batten walls of light pine with generous windows (opposite) surround the masonry fireplace core as well as define the exterior (pages 20–21).

HANNA (HONEYCOMB) HOUSE

PALO ALTO, CALIFORNIA. 1936

TWO THOUSAND MILES AWAY, ANOTHER pioneering couple, Paul and Jean Hanna, built a completely different type of Usonian house. Their 4,825-square-foot home grew from a hillside near Stanford University, where Paul Hanna was a professor. Based on a hexagonal module that is 2'2" on a side, the house seems to ramble casually around the hill using 60- and 120-degree angles. The roofs are pitched, not flat, and so are more compatible with the open angles of a hexagon.

A honeycomb grid establishes the plan, which carried Wright one more step away from traditional rectangular boxes toward the circular plans of his later years. It is an embracing shape that creates a variety of interior spaces that gradually reveal and then conceal themselves. The Wright-designed furnishings are drawn from the hexagonal motif, thus tying the freestanding elements to those built in. The grass matting covering the changing levels of the ceiling lends a neutral texture to the smoothness of the board-and-glass walls.

In 1974 the Hannas passed ownership of their treasure to Stanford University.

⸭ All corners are obtuse as in the honeycombs, therefore a pattern more natural to human movement is the result. ⸭

Frank Lloyd Wright
Architectural Record, 1938

Rather than move when their family needs changed, the Hannas took advantage of the screenlike quality of the walls and simply rearranged spaces. They also added a guesthouse, garden house, and hobby shop.

The openness of the Hanna house to the gardens enriches both, creating a decidedly Japanese feeling. The elaborate brick walls and terraces have been enhanced by years of sympathetic landscaping.

P O P E - L E I G H E Y   H O U S E

Narrow windows in the cypress walls have perforated plywood screens with an abstract design (opposite). Filtering light as branches do sunlight, they create delicate shadow patterns.

Modular Usonian furniture (page 28) could be arranged to suit multiple uses. Simple plywood chairs were grouped around individual tables for cards, around a long table for dinner parties, or in clusters for conversation. Hallways (page 29) were narrow to save space.

IN YET A DIFFERENT PART OF THE country, another journalist (like Herbert Jacobs in Wisconsin) approached Wright about designing a small home for his family. And like the Jacobses' house, Loren and Charlotte Pope's home was based on a rectangular module but had just 1,200 square feet of space and cost $8,000 to construct. It proved to be brilliantly simple—a spiritually enriching environment that eliminated all that was unnecessary.

This version of the familiar L-shaped plan allowed the living-dining area to open on both sides. The fireplace, backed by the workspace and service core, provides an anchor for the lightness of the surrounding walls. Subtle changes in level of the warm red, concrete floor suggest changes in the use of the open spaces.

When a proposed highway threatened the house, second owner Marjorie Leighey donated it to the National Trust for Historic Preservation in 1964 so that it could be saved. It was disassembled and rebuilt at historic Woodlawn Plantation, providing a contrast in two centuries of American housing.

GOETSCH-WINCKLER HOUSE

The graceful, restful house crests a rise on the wooded site (opposite). From the initial approach beneath a wide, sheltering eave, down the length of the house, the horizontal emphasis is clear. Three levels of flat roof float over the redwood walls and brick piers.

Rows of casement windows (pages 32–33) open the two long sides of the house to terraces, lawn, and woods. The end is closed, creating a protected space by the fire.

ALMA GOETSCH AND KATHERINE WINCKLER were part of a group of seven teachers from Michigan State University who asked Wright to design them a community of houses around a farm unit on a forty-acre plot. If the Federal Housing Administration had authorized the loans, it would have been Wright's first planned community. Unfortunately, the cooperative plan was abandoned, but the women persisted and had their Usonian home completed by 1940.

The house is a compact, single-block plan. The workspace is not at the "hinge" location between living and sleeping areas but at one end, behind the living room fireplace. The small bedrooms and bath are at the other end. It is an efficient 1,350-square-foot house built on a four-foot-square module. An alcove in the living room provides an intimate gathering place by the fireplace in an otherwise open room. Changes in usage for different parts of the living space are suggested by the architecture but not dictated by separate rooms, preserving the freedom and flexibility that are hallmarks of Wright's Usonian designs.

A F F L E C K   H O U S E

A MORE DRAMATIC VARIATION OF THE Usonian house was the raised form, which was suitable for more challenging sites. The steeply sloping, wooded lot with a meandering stream selected by Elizabeth and Gregor Affleck, a fellow Wisconsinite and an engineer, inspired this approach.

Cantilevered over the ravine, the house soars through the treetops. Views are skillfully interwoven into the house. The loggia is a transition to the inside, barely enclosed. It is open above through skylights, below through a well and a stairway leading to the garden, and beyond through a row of casement windows framing views of the woods. The cypress boards, all custom milled to overlap properly, were skillfully assembled to cover the sandwich walls inside and out, creating a horizontally textured skin over the geometric sculpture. The forty-foot living area is nestled in the trees like a tree house, overlooking the ravine. The workspace is behind it, and the bedroom wing is perpendicular to it.

Wright fit this home into its site as naturally as if it had grown there.

The Affleck house was built by master craftsman Harold Turner, who adeptly converted innovative Wright drawings into numerous well-built Usonian homes.

Masonry walls confirm the house's horizontal tie to the earth while anchoring the whole. At 2,350 square feet, the L-shaped plan with a square grid was a bit larger than many and had more special features and details, making it more costly ($19,000). The house is now owned by Lawrence Institute of Technology.

PALMER HOUSE

WHEN WILLIAM AND MARY PALMER asked Wright to design them a home near the University of Michigan campus where William Palmer taught, they sought the life-enriching experience his houses promised. The result was a successful marriage of architect, client, and site. Based on a triangular module, the house was composed as carefully as a symphony and has been masterfully tended by the Palmers for more than forty years.

The entrance to the house gradually unfolds. Once inside, the living area in the primary triangle opens dramatically to the Japanese-influenced garden beyond, the extended roofline nearly pointing the way. A narrow passageway leads to the bedroom wing, located in a second triangle. The angles create partial hexagons and parallelograms of space, all responding to the grid in the waxed, red concrete floor. Clear-grained red tidewater cypress boards rise to the ceiling.

The terrace, partially covered by broad eaves, is merely an extension of the interior space. The sense of Japanese simplicity, of repose and harmony, radiates from every part of the house.

Working with former Wright associate John Howe, in 1964 the Palmers built a triangular garden house nearby that repeats the module and style of the main house (opposite).

Warm autumn colors and Japanese textiles (pages 38–39) complement the simple furniture that was designed as part of the composition for living.

ZIMMERMAN HOUSE

ISADORE AND LUCILLE ZIMMERMAN were disillusioned with their traditional house and began to read extensively about alternative solutions to the housing dilemma. A professional couple with no children, they, like Wright, were devoted to art and music. Fortunately, they discovered Wright's autobiography and quickly decided that he was their architect.

A partially exposed rock on the wooded site became a focal point at the front entrance. The house, now owned and restored by the Currier Gallery of Art, has an in-line plan, compact and handcrafted like a fine piece of furniture. Every detail, including the garden and even linens, was specially designed for it.

Wright customarily assigned an apprentice as the site supervisor for his Usonian houses. John Geiger was sent to help the Zimmermans and actually lived with them until construction was completed. He made many decisions on the spot but contacted Taliesin for permission on others. With many buildings such as the Zimmerman house, these young architects guided Wright's visionary, unconventional designs to completion.

The living room, called the garden room, was appointed with a Wright-designed quartet stand suitable for the Zimmermans' concert evenings. Two small bedrooms are tucked privately behind the workspace.

· 41

⚏ This Usonian dwelling seems a thing loving the ground with a new sense of space, light, and freedom — to which our U.S.A. is entitled. ⚏

Frank Lloyd Wright
The Natural House, 1954

While clearly Usonian in plan and concept, the Zimmerman house has a somewhat Prairie Style feel, with its long, low, red-tile hipped roof, masonry walls, and pure rectilinear character.

REISLEY HOUSE

PLEASANTVILLE, NEW YORK . 1951

THE CURVING, PICTURESQUE ROADS of Usonia, Wright's largest planned community, shelter forty-eight residences, half of them designed by Wright or his apprentices. Wright's last design here was for a young physicist, Roland Reisley, and his wife, Ronny.

Built of cypress and granite gathered from the site and a quarry nearby, the house is an extension of the land. The stone was laid naturally as it was found—the soaring, angular but horizontal rooflines sheltering all. The terrace, a triangular extension of the living room, is formed by stone walls rising from the hillside. An angle of 120 degrees, not the familiar 90, creates a dynamic plan. Rather than being stopped by a perpendicular wall, one is gently guided around the house.

In keeping with Wright's hope that Usonian houses would respond to changing needs, the Reisleys nearly doubled their 1,800-square-foot house in 1956. One arm of the overlapping triangular plan was merely extended—enhancing, not weakening, the harmonious design. The expansion increased the living space and allowed the house to grow along with the family.

The Reisleys' house exemplifies Usonian characteristics, yet it is larger and more complex than many. Still faithful to Wright's design, it has been carefully maintained and appreciated by its original owners for more than four decades.

The house's triangular
module forms hexagonal and
parallelogram shapes from
which furniture rises;
light decks float above.
The expansion created a
separate dining area and
added four generously sized
bedrooms and a bath.

ROBERT LLEWELLYN WRIGHT HOUSE

BETHESDA, MARYLAND. 1953

WHEN WRIGHT DESIGNED A HOME for his youngest son, a Washington lawyer, he completely broke away from the traditional boxlike forms. Both his first and second schemes for Robert Llewellyn and Elizabeth Wright were based on the circle. The elliptical shape of the final scheme offers—like the sweep of an extended arm—open living spaces and the woods beyond.

Similar to the solar hemicycle home he designed for the Jacobs family in 1944, the house has an efficient two-story plan with bedrooms above the curved living spaces. For it Wright used concrete block—not patterned like his earlier textile blocks or Usonian Automatic blocks, but standard flat block. Laid in curves, the solid material appears plastic and fluid as it molds the spaces. The lapped Philippine mahogany boards that wrap the upper walls add to the horizontal fluidity of the design and provide warmth. All ornament is a result of the manipulation of the materials, the rhythm of the boards, and the clerestory window patterns created by the blocks.

Despite the hard surfaces of concrete floors and walls, the house is an inviting and cozy shelter.

▓ Every house worth considering as a work of art must have a grammar of its own. ▓

Frank Lloyd Wright
The Natural House, 1954

The house is both simple and complex, as partial circles intersect to create curious but embracing rooms. Circular forms are repeated in the furnishings that Wright designed for the house.

The street side of the house is closed and private, with only small windows admitting light. The southern exposure, in contrast, is open to a delightful curved terrace and a balcony nestled in the trees. Unlike most Usonians, the house does not have a carport or radiant heat.

TRACY HOUSE

ONE OF WRIGHT'S MOST DELIGHTFUL Usonian Automatic houses was designed for structural engineer William Tracy and his wife, Elizabeth. Beginning with the American System Built homes of 1915 and then the textile-block houses of the 1920s, Wright experimented with various standardized building techniques. His hope that the Usonian Automatic houses of specially cast concrete blocks could be assembled inexpensively by the owners proved unworkable, but the concept and the seven prototypes built after 1950 were visionary.

The compact L plan of the 1,200-square-foot Tracy house sits on a breathtaking site high above Puget Sound. Taking their cue from the site, the concrete shapes build from gently rising stairs to the garden walls to the walls of the house itself. The inherent ornament in the various block shapes creates a harmonious rhythm throughout. The lines are crisp and sculptural. Three small bedrooms are on the street side, while the combination living-dining space stretches across the front and opens to a terrace. All excess has been eliminated in this simple and perfectly integrated shelter.

▪▪ The enclosed space within them is the *reality* of the building. ▪▪   Frank Lloyd Wright
The Natural House, 1954

Usonian Automatic owners were given a set of forms from which to cast the different hollow block shapes necessary to build walls, ceilings, and windows, all to be tied together with a mesh of steel rods and erected on a concrete pad. Close supervision of this project led to a finely engineered structure.

Wright signed this
experimental composition
with his standard red
ceramic tile. The house's
mitered glass corners demate-
rialize the solidity of the
concrete building material,
leaving an outline instead.

Hanna, Paul and Jean. *Frank Lloyd Wright's Hanna House: The Client's Report.* Architectural History Foundation. Cambridge: MIT Press, 1981.

Henken, Priscilla and David. *Realizations of Usonia: Frank Lloyd Wright in Westchester.* Yonkers, New York: Hudson River Museum, 1985.

Hitchcock, Henry-Russell. *In the Nature of Materials: The Buildings of Frank Lloyd Wright, 1887–1941.* 1942. Reprint. New York: Da Capo Press, 1969.

Pfeiffer, Bruce Brooks, ed. *Frank Lloyd Wright Monographs.* Vols. 6, 7, 8. Tokyo: ADA Edita, 1987.

———. *Frank Lloyd Wright Selected Houses.* Vols. 5, 6, 7. Tokyo: ADA Edita, 1990–91.

Rosenbaum, Alvin. *Usonia: Frank Lloyd Wright's Design for America.* Washington, D.C.: Preservation Press, 1993.

Sergeant, John. *Frank Lloyd Wright's Usonian Houses: A Case for Organic Architecture.* New York: Whitney Library of Design, Watson-Guptill, 1976.

Wright, Frank Lloyd. *The Natural House.* New York: Bramhall House, 1954.

The author wishes to thank the owners of the Usonian houses featured here, especially original clients Katherine Jacobs, Mary and William Palmer, Loren Pope, Ronny and Roland Reisley, Mildred Rosenbaum, Elizabeth and William Tracy, and Elizabeth Wright. Appreciation is also due David Greeff for assistance with new photography of the Goetsch-Winckler house.

The cover illustration by Robert L. Wiser is adapted from a photograph by Jack E. Boucher, Historic American Buildings Survey.

Illustration Sources:
Ping Amranand: 14 top right, 26, 28, 29
Gordon Beall: 45, 46, 47
© Wayne Cable, Cable Studios: 18, 20–21
Currier Gallery of Art, Manchester, N.H.; bequest of Isadore J. and Lucille Zimmerman: 40, 42–43

Pedro E. Guerrero: 1, 10, 11, 17 top right
Carol M. Highsmith: 6–7, 8
Historic American Buildings Survey: 27
Balthazar Korab Ltd.: 12, 14 top left, 17 top left, 17 bottom left, 24, 31, 32–33, 35, 36, 38–39
Andrew D. Lautman: 48, 50, 51
Ezra Stoller © Esto: 17 bottom right, 23
Scot Zimmerman: 2, 14 bottom left and right, 25, 53, 54, 55